REVOLUTION!

REVOLUTION!

SAYINGS OF
VLADIMIR LENIN

Bodleian Library

INTRODUCTION

Every revolution needs its spokesmen or women. While perhaps the most polished orator of the Russian Revolution was Leon Trotsky, it is the voice of Vladimir Lenin, the architect of the Revolution, which rings out through history as the authentic call to arms against the tyranny of *anciens régimes* everywhere.

Lenin knew how to galvanize crowds. He fixed his audience with a penetrating stare and paced purposefully on the platform. His fingers instinctively clutched the edge of the podium as he leaned forward, giving the impression – and authority – of a natural teacher. Yet his rhetorical skills were limited by his awkward manner and stocky appearance. He took time to gather momentum in his speeches and even then never overcame his inability to pronounce properly the letter 'r'. This apparent rusticity gave him an air of self-conviction in the eyes of the masses, reinforcing his credibility and authority.

Morgan Philips Price, the *Manchester Guardian* correspondent, who heard Lenin speak, recalled: 'No uncertain words came from his lips. Straight to the point he went from the first moment of his speech and pursued his opponents with merciless logic.'[1]

Lenin's contemporary, Nikolai Sukhanov, described Lenin as 'a thunderous orator' who would pound home his arguments with a relentless logic that enslaved his listeners.[2]

It was this quality which Josef Stalin recalled on first hearing Lenin. 'I was captivated by that irresistible force of logic...which, although somewhat terse, gained a firm hold on his audience, gradually electrified it, and then, as one might say, completely overpowered it.'[3]

This driving power is also evident in his writing. Lenin captivated readers with the sheer force of his arguments. He heightened their effect through the use of apocalyptic language and hard-hitting descriptions of the perceived adversaries of Marxism. He wrote with the assurance of a natural leader, mesmerizing even those who did not agree with him. He cast the struggle of the age as one fundamentally of class and advocated the necessity of ruthless, violent measures. He expressed these ideas with such clarity and brevity and force as to create a body of eminently quotable quotations, long before the age of the sound bite.

Lenin's role as orator of revolution is witnessed by the many unverified and dubious revolutionary quotations attributed to him circulating on the Internet – a fate he shares with many standard bearers of diverse causes, whose preeminent positions are illicitly used to authorize new works. This little volume, culled from the vast 45-volume work *The Collected Works of V.I. Lenin* (Moscow, 1927) via the Marxists Internet Archive, gathers some of Lenin's most memorable sayings. Together, these give a glimpse into the rhetorical power and conviction of a man whose name has become synonymous with the October Revolution and who remains the embodiment of the idea of revolution.

1. Morgan Philips Price, *My Reminiscences of the Russian Revolution* (London, 1921), pp. 43–6.

2. *The Russian Revolution 1917: A Personal Record by N.N. Sukhanov*, ed. and tr. Joel Carmichael (Oxford, 1955), p. 284.

3. J.V. Stalin, 'Lenin', in *Works* (Moscow, 1954), Vol. 6, January–November, 1924, pp. 54–66, consulted via Marxists Internet Archive.

'Revolution can
never be forecast;
it cannot be foretold;
it comes of itself.
Revolution is brewing
and is bound to flare up.'

Drive Red Wedges in White Troops. Soviet
propaganda poster by Lazar Lissitzky, 1920.

'The oppressed are allowed once every few years to decide which particular representatives of the oppressing class shall represent and repress them in parliament!'

'It is not difficult to be a revolutionary when revolution has already broken out and is in spate, when all people are joining the revolution just because they are carried away, because it is the vogue...It is far more difficult – and far more precious – to be a revolutionary when the conditions for direct, open, really mass and really revolutionary struggle *do not yet exist*.'

Nevsky Prospekt, Petrograd, July 1917.

'The bourgeoisie incites the workers of one nation against those of another in the endeavour to keep them disunited.'

Friendship of the nations, 1923.
Detail of a painting by Stepan Karpov.

'Human child birth is an act which transforms the woman into an almost lifeless, bloodstained heap of flesh, tortured, tormented and driven frantic by pain.'

'The class struggle did not accidentally assume its latest form, the form in which the exploited class takes all the means of power in its own hands in order to completely destroy its class enemy, the bourgeoisie.'

Soviet poster for the Third International, 1925.

LONG LIVE THE THIRD
COMMUNIST INTERNATIONAL!
VVIVA IL TERZA
INTERNAZIONALE COMMUNISTA!

VIVE LA
INTERNATIONA
ES LEBE
KOMMUNISTISCH

'We would be deceiving both ourselves and the people if we concealed from the masses the necessity of a desperate, bloody war of extermination, as the immediate task of the coming revolutionary action.'

'Not a single problem of the class struggle has ever been solved in history except by violence.'

'You cannot do anything without rousing the masses to action.'

Lenin on a tribune by
Alexander Gerasimov, 1930.

'You must act with all energy.
Mass searches.
Execution for concealing arms.'

'Surely you do not imagine that we shall be victorious without applying the most cruel revolutionary terror?'

Anti-White Army poster, 1917, with the caption: 'Enemy at the gates! Everyone to the defence'.

ВРАГ У ВОРОТ!!!

ВСЕ НА ЗАЩИТУ

Undated poster featuring Lenin with the slogan, 'Long live the Socialist revolution!'

'When violence is exercised by the working people, by the mass of exploited against the exploiters – then we are for it!'

'We can't expect to get anywhere unless we resort to terrorism: speculators must be shot on the spot. Moreover, bandits must be dealt with just as resolutely: they must be shot on the spot.'

'…when people charge us with harshness we wonder how they can forget the rudiments of Marxism.'

'No mercy for these enemies of the people, the enemies of socialism, the enemies of the working people! War to the death against the rich and their hangers-on, the bourgeois intellectuals; war on the rogues, the idlers and the rowdies!'

'You need to hang (hang without fail, so that the people see) no fewer than 100 of the notorious kulaks, the rich, and the bloodsuckers.'

'I can't listen to music too often. It affects your nerves, makes you want to say stupid nice things and stroke the heads of people who could create such beauty while living in this vile hell.'

Detail from *Lamp and Musical Instruments* by Kazimir Malevich, 1913.

'It is necessary –
secretly and *urgently*
to prepare the terror.'

**Poster of Lenin with the slogans, 'Land to the peasants',
'Peace to the nations', 'Power to the Soviets' (undated).**

'When a liberal is abused, he says, "Thank God they didn't beat me." When he is beaten, he thanks God they didn't kill him. When he is killed, he will thank God that his immortal soul has been delivered from its mortal clay.'

'Imperialism:
the highest
stage of
capitalism.'

Postcard produced by the
A.F. Postnov factory in 1917
following the overthrow of the Tsar.

'The worker is becoming impoverished absolutely, i.e., he is actually becoming poorer than before; he is compelled to live worse, to eat worse, to suffer hunger more, and to live in basements and attics.'

'Freedom in capitalist society always remains about the same as it was in the ancient Greek republics: freedom for the slave-owners.'

'Democracy for an insignificant minority, democracy for the rich – that is the democracy of capitalist society.'

Poster with the caption, 'Those who are against the Soviets', 1917.

'Present-day society is wholly based on the exploitation of the vast masses of the working class by a tiny minority of the population, the class of the landowners and that of the capitalists. It is a slave society, since the "free" workers, who all their life work for the capitalists, are "entitled" only to such means of subsistence as are essential for the maintenance of slaves who produce profit, for the safeguarding and perpetuation of capitalist slavery.'

'Capitalism has triumphed all over the world, but this triumph is only the prelude to the triumph of labour over capital.'

Illustration for magazine cover, *c.*1920.

'...let the bourgeoisie rage and fume, but only people who shut their eyes so as not to see, and stuff their ears so as not to hear, can fail to notice that all over the world the birth pangs of the old, capitalist society, which is pregnant with socialism, have begun.'

'Welcome comrades', poster
by D. Moor, *c.*1920.

'The bourgeoisie are today evading taxation by bribery and through their connections; we must close all loopholes.'

'The intellectual forces of the workers and peasants are growing and getting stronger in their fight to overthrow the bourgeoisie and their accomplices, the educated classes, the lackeys of capital, who consider themselves the brains of the nation. In fact they are not its brains but its shit.'

'Illiterate man is a blind man', Soviet poster to encourage education.

'America has become one of the foremost countries in regard to the depth of the abyss which lies between the handful of arrogant multimillionaires who wallow in filth and luxury, and the millions of working people who constantly live on the verge of pauperism.'

'Under socialism all will govern in turn and will soon become accustomed to no one governing.'

'Without revolutionary theory there can be no revolutionary movement.'

Abstract Composition by Olga Rozanova, 1910.

'All over the world, wherever there are capitalists, freedom of the press means freedom to buy up newspapers, to buy writers, to bribe, buy and fake "public opinion" for the benefit of the bourgeoisie.'

Poster to commemorate 1 May with a quote from the *Communist Manifesto*: 'The proletarians have nothing to lose but their chains. They have a world to win.'

'A newspaper is not only a collective propagandist and a collective agitator, it is also a collective organizer.'

'Discrimination among citizens on account of their religious convictions is wholly intolerable. Even the bare mention of a citizen's religion in official documents should unquestionably be eliminated.'

'Human knowledge is not (or does not follow) a straight line, but a curve, which endlessly approximates a series of circles, a spiral.'

Vladimir Tatlin's *Monument to the Third International*, Petrograd 1920.

'Unity is a great thing and a great slogan. But what the workers' cause needs is the *unity of Marxists*, not unity between Marxists, and opponents and distorters of Marxism.'

'The art of any propagandist and agitator consists in his ability to find the best means of influencing any given audience, by presenting a definite truth, in such a way as to make it most convincing, most easy to digest, most graphic, and most strongly impressive.'

Bronze statue of Lenin in Moscow.

'Russia achieved Marxism –
the only correct revolutionary
theory – through the agony she
experienced in the course of half
a century of unparalleled torment
and sacrifice, of unparalleled
revolutionary heroism, incredible
energy, devoted searching, study,
practical trial, disappointment,
verification, and comparison with
European experience.'

'The revolution does not need historians.'

OKTOBRA KAROGU
SARGĀSIM MŪŽOS

'War cannot be abolished unless classes are abolished and socialism is created.'

'We fully regard civil wars, i.e., wars waged by the oppressed class against the oppressing class, slaves against slave-owners, serfs against land-owners, and wage-workers against the bourgeoisie, as legitimate, progressive and necessary.'

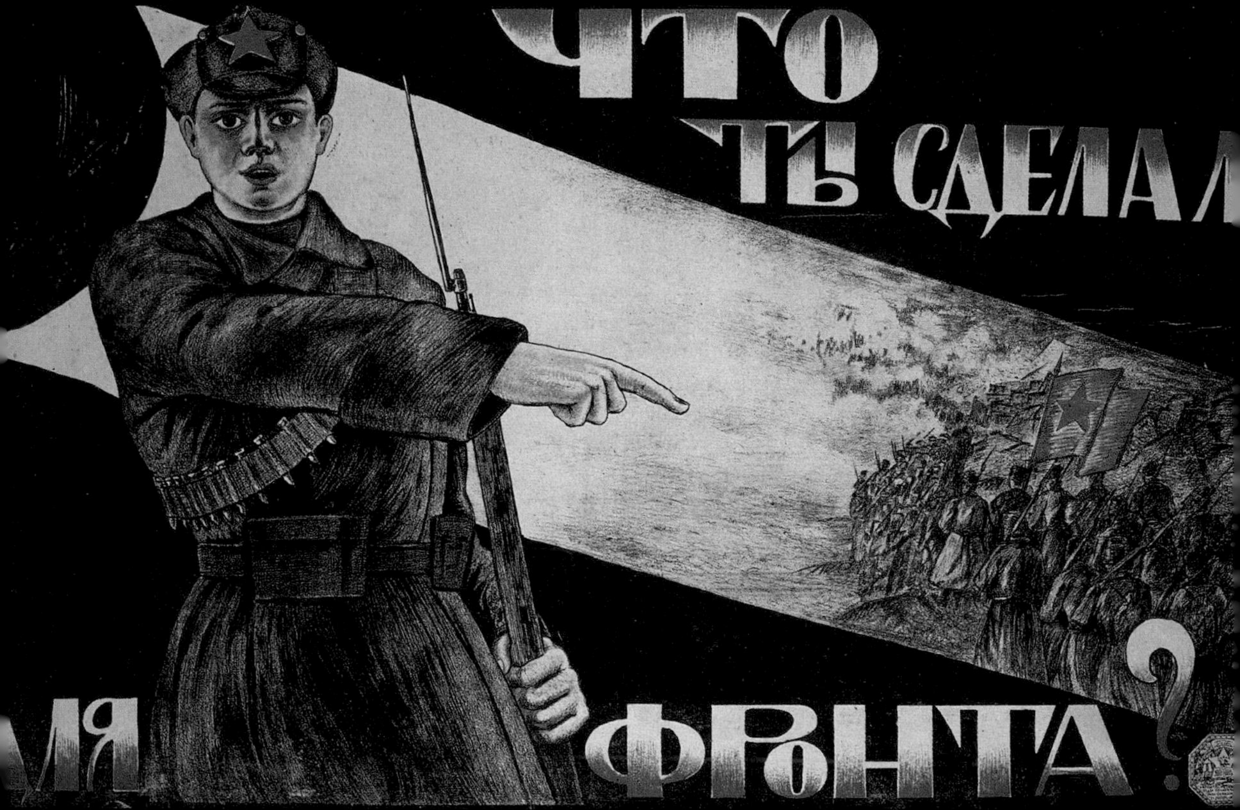
ЧТО
ТЫ СДЕЛАЛ
ФРОНТА?

'It is at moments of need that one learns who one's friends are. Defeated armies learn their lesson.'

'Comrade Stalin, having become Secretary-General, has unlimited authority concentrated in his hands, and I am not sure whether he will always be capable of using that authority with sufficient caution.'

Portrait of Stalin, undated.

'The functionaries of our political organizations and trade unions are corrupted – or rather tend to be corrupted – by the conditions of capitalism and betray a tendency to become bureaucrats, i.e., privileged persons divorced from the people and standing above the people.'

The Duma after the February Revolution, 1917.

'Comrade Trotsky...is distinguished not only by outstanding ability. He is personally perhaps the most capable man in the present C.C. [Central Committee]...'

Leon Trotsky, *c.*1920.

'The proletarian state has to forcibly move a very poor family into a rich man's flat.'

Villagers read Lenin's decree concerning land redistribution (published 26 October 1917). Illustration undated.

'The salaries of all officials, all of whom are elective and displaceable at any time, not to exceed the average wage of a competent worker.'

'A party is the vanguard of a class, and its duty is to lead the masses and not merely to reflect the average political level of the masses.'

'Attention must be devoted *principally to raising* the workers to the level of revolutionaries; it is not at all our task *to descend to* the level of the "working masses".'

Lenin in the Kremlin, 1920. Reproduction of a painting by V. Ivanov.

'Not a single bourgeois state, not even the most progressive, republican democratic state, has brought about complete equality of rights. But the Soviet Republic of Russia promptly wiped out, *without any exception*, every trace of inequality in the legal status of women, and secured her complete equality in its laws.'

Detail from a poster with the slogan, 'The immortal October leader Lenin has shown us the way to victory; long live Leninism', 1925.

ЧТОБЫ БОЛЬШЕ ПРОИЗВОДИТЬ- НАДО БОЛЬШЕ ЗНАТЬ

'Up to now the peasant has been compelled to loan grain to the workers' state; the pieces of coloured paper called money received in return for grain do not satisfy the peasant.'

Soviet poster with the slogan, 'In order to have more, it is necessary to produce more. In order to produce more, it is necessary to know more'. By Alexander Zelensky, 1920.

'Despair is typical
of those who do
not understand
the causes of evil,
see no way out,
and are incapable
of struggle.'

Picture Credits

References

Unless specified, quotations are taken from *The Collected Works of V.I. Lenin*, Progress Publishers, Moscow, 1960–80. An online edition of this work is available at Marxists Internet Archive, www.marxists.org.

6 *Collected Works*, vol. 28, p. 83.
9 'The State and Revolution' (1917) in *Collected Works*, vol. 25, pp. 381–492.
10 *Collected Works*, vol. 31, pp. 117–18.
13 *Collected Works*, vol. 19, pp. 454–7.
14 'Prophetic Words' (1918) in *Collected Works*, vol. 27, pp. 494–9.
16 'Report on the Activities of the Council of People's Commissars' (1918) in *Collected Works*, vol. 26, pp. 459–61.
18 'Lessons of the Moscow Uprising', *Collected Works*, vol. 11, p. 174.
21 'Report on the Activities of the Council of People's Commissars' (1918) in *Collected Works*, vol. 26, pp. 459–61.
22 *Collected Works*, vol. 26, pp. 501–2.
24 'Letter to G.F. Fyodorov' (1918) in *Collected Works*, vol. 35, p. 349.
26 Quoted in Legett, George, *The Cheka: Lenin's Political Police*, p. 57, Oxford University Press, Oxford, 1981.
29 Report on the 'Activities of the Council of People's Commissars', *Collected Works*, vol. 26, pp. 459–61.
30 'Meeting of the Presidium of the Petrograd Soviet With Delegates From the Food Supply Organisations' in *Collected Works*, vol. 26, p. 501.
33 *Collected Works*, vol. 28, pp. 169–70.
34 *Collected Works*, vol. 26, pp. 404–15.
36 Telegram to Comrades Kuraev, Bosh, Minkin, and other Penza communists, 11 August, 1918.
39 Quoted in King, Terry, *Gregor Piatigorsky: The Life and Career of the Virtuoso Cellist*, p. 14, McFarland & Co Inc., 2010.

40 Quoted in Vasili Mitrokhin Christopher and Andrew Vasili Mitrokhin, *The Mitrokhin Archive: The KGB in Europe and the West*, p. 34, Gardners Books, London, 2000.
43 *Collected Works*, vol. 11, pp. 383–8.
45 'Imperialism: The Highest Stage of Capitalism' (1914) in *Collected Works*, vol. 22, pp. 185–298.
46 'Impoverishment in Capitalist Society' in *Collected Works*, vol. 18, pp. 435–6.
48 'The State and Revolution' (1917) in *Collected Works*, vol. 25, pp. 381–492.
51 'The State and Revolution' (1917) in *Collected Works*, vol. 25, pp. 381–492.
52 'Socialism and Religion' in *Collected Works*, vol. 10, pp. 83–7.
54 'The Three Sources and Three Component Parts of Marxism' (1913) in *Collected Works*, vol. 19, pp. 21–8.
57 'Prophetic Words' (1918) in *Collected Works*, vol. 27, pp. 494–9.
58 'Report to the All Russia Congress of Representatives of Financial Departments of Soviets', *Collected Works*, vol. 27, pp. 383–7.
61 Letter from Lenin to Gorky, 15 September, 1919, Library of Congress, Russian Archives.
62 'Letter to American Workers', *Collected Works*, vol. 28, pp. 62–75.
65 'The State and Revolution' (1917) in *Collected Works*, vol. 25, pp. 381–492.
66 'What Is To Be Done?' (1901–2) in *Collected Works*, vol. 5, pp. 347–530.
69 'Letter to G. Myasnikov' in *Collected Works*, vol. 32, pp. 504–9.
70 'What Is To Be Done?' (1901–2) in *Collected Works*, vol. 5, pp. 347–530.
72 'Socialism and Religion' in *Collected Works*, vol. 10, pp. 83–7.

75 'Summary of Dialectics' (1914) in *Collected Works*, vol. 38, pp. 220–2.
76 *Collected Works*, vol. 20, pp. 230–2.
79 'The Slogans and Organisation of Social-Democratic Work' (1919) in *Collected Works*, vol. 17, pp. 331–41.
80 'Left-Wing Communism: An Infantile Disorder' (1920) in *Collected Works*, vol. 31, pp. 117–18.
82 Quoted in Perry, J.C., and Constantine V. Pleshakov, *The Flight Of The Romanovs: A Family Saga*, p. 209, Basic Books, New York, 1999.
85 'Socialism and War' (1915) in *Collected Works*, vol. 21, pp. 295–338.
86 'Socialism and War' (1915) in *Collected Works*, vol. 21, pp. 295–338.
89 'Left-Wing Communism: An Infantile Disorder' (1920) in *Collected Works*, vol. 31, pp. 117–18.
90 'Letter to the Congress' (1922) in *Collected Works*, vol. 36, pp. 593–611.
93 'The State and Revolution', in *Collected Works*, vol. 25, pp. 381–492.
94 'Letter to the Congress' (1922) in *Collected Works*, vol. 36, pp. 593–611.
97 'Can the Bolsheviks retain state power?' in *Collected Works*, pp. 87–136.
99 'April Theses' (1917) in *Collected Works*, vol. 24, pp. 19–26.
100 'Speech On The Agrarian Question' (1917) in *Collected Works*, vol. 26, pp. 321–32.
103 'What Is To Be Done?' (1901–2) in *Collected Works*, vol. 5, pp. 347–530.
104 Quoted in *Women and Communism*, Lawrence & Wishart, London, 1950.
107 *Collected Works*, vol. 30, pp. 374–9.
108 'L.N. Tolstoy and the Modern Labour Movement' (1910) in *Collected Works*, vol. 16, pp. 330–2.

First published in 2017 by the Bodleian Library
Broad Street, Oxford OX1 3BG

www.bodleianshop.co.uk

ISBN: 978 1 85124 470 6

Selection and arrangement © Bodleian Library, University of Oxford, 2017
Images, unless specified on p. 110 © Bodleian Library, University of Oxford, 2017
All rights reserved

Picture research by Leanda Shrimpton
The publisher would like to thank Irina Baysheva and
Naomi Polonsky for their help with this book
Cover design by Dot Little at the Bodleian Library
Designed and typeset by Karin Fremer in ITC Franklin Gothic
Printed and bound by Great Wall Printing Co. Ltd., Hong Kong on 157gsm Chen Ming

British Library Catalogue in Publishing Data
A CIP record of this publication is available from the British Library